"The quest for knowledge and insight is like climbing a mountain. You start alone among the trees and ravines. Then as you get to the heights, you see others who have been climbing different routes yet getting to the same place. Dennis Stauffer has found a great route to understanding the thinking processes that lead to innovation and change, as well as the process that stalls people into stagnant spirals.

Thinking Clockwise is concise, easy to read, and packed with insights, wisdom, and examples of how people think and why some environments facilitate change, while others poison it."

—Art Fry,
Inventor of Post-It Notes

THINKING CLOCKWISE

A FIELD GUIDE FOR THE INNOVATIVE LEADER

Published by MinneApplePress
P.O. Box 46021, Minneapolis, Minnesota, 55446

Clockwise is a trademark owned by Dennis Stauffer and used here by permission. To obtain permission to use Clockwise with appropriate attribution, contact MinneApplePress.

Library of Congress Control Number: 2004107511

ISBN:0-9640429-3-2 (Hardcover)

Cover design by Mark Dame   Interior layout by Allison Pickett

Text Editing by Linda Rening, Amy Farrar, and John Stauffer

Printed in the United States of America

Dedicated to Ben and Beth.
May you always find amazement.

Contents

Have you ever wished you were more creative and insightful? Have you ever been frustrated by the way someone seems to think? Have you ever wished you could better explain a concept to someone or grasp it more easily yourself?

Haven't we all?

We all think and reason. We all come up with ideas. But how do we know if those ideas will work, or if they're even worth pursuing? Which ideas reflect true understanding?

What does it mean to say we *know* something?

Great philosophers have struggled with that question for thousands of years and I don't pretend to have the final answer. What I offer is a simple yet powerful technique you can use immediately to gain new and innovative insights.

Still, thinking innovatively isn't enough. It is just as important to create a *climate* that promotes this sort of thinking—an environment that scales it up from the individual to a team, a unit, or an entire organization. That's the leadership component. The full power of this model comes when it is used to create a *culture* of innovation.

As you read this book, it may occur to you that this model has implications beyond the spheres of leadership, business innovation, and organizational behavior. While I don't attempt to cover all of those implications here, I hope you will use this model wherever it makes sense to you to do so.

This is not a book of science or philosophy. Rather, as the name suggests, this is a field guide such as a naturalist might use to observe wildlife. It provides a combination of observations and insights that explain what to look for as you make your own observations, and it helps you to interpret those observations.

In so doing, it explains how to be more creative in practical ways, how to approach problems more productively, and how to cultivate that type of thinking and creativity among those around you. In short, it's designed to be a simple user-friendly guide to innovative thinking and leadership.

Considerable scientific research in a wide range of fields supports these concepts. While I find it compelling, I recognize that not everyone shares my fascination with those details, so I haven't cited them. As you read about these concepts and reflect on your own experience, I believe they will ring as true to you as they have to me.

Part One: Clockwise Thinking

Insight Trumps Knowledge

Most of us spend our lives pursuing knowledge when what we really need is insight. Throughout our education and our careers we strive to learn things that we hope will bring us success. While knowledge is certainly important, a great insight will beat it every time.

For example:

People had been experimenting with electricity for well over a century and researchers all over the world understood how it worked; *one* of them invented the light bulb and the infastructure that made it viable.

Many companies knew how to make automobiles—and were doing it very profitably; a guy named Ford started doing it on an assembly line.

Many companies were selling cosmetics when one woman decided to do it in a way that provided non-traditional jobs to other women, selling to women. She created Mary Kay.

Sears and K-Mart were once two of the most successful retailers in the world. They knew their business, until a company in rural Arkansas began selling in places those companies considered too small to bother with and Wal-Mart overtook them.

IBM understood the computer business like no one else in the world—or so it thought. So it gave what it considered to be the least profitable part of a new venture to a fledgling company called Microsoft.

Thousands of entrepreneurs saw dollar signs on the Internet; one realized that the way to leverage that new medium was with, of all things, books. He called it Amazon.com.

Thomas Edison, Henry Ford, Mary Kay Ash, Sam Walton, Bill Gates, Jeff Bezos. They're just a tiny fraction of all the examples one could give of people whose insight trumped everyone else's knowledge. Any business school graduate could quickly list many more.

It's no different inside organizations. Does anyone who has worked in a large company more than a few months believe that promotions go to those who "know" the most? (And even when they do, is that always good?)

One of business' greatest truisms is that you must know your customer. Yet you can know your customer quite well and still get thumped in the marketplace—by someone who has figured out something that even your customers don't yet know about themselves. (See above list.)

Knowledge is not only less powerful than insight; there are times when what we think we know can become one of our greatest obstacles. (IBM, Sears. . .)

If some genie ever offers you a choice between profound knowledge and profound insight, choose insight. Those who have not yet been given that option, read on.

FIELD NOTES:

Innovation requires insight.

This book is based on a simple metaphor for effective thinking, a pattern that also defines important principles of leadership, especially leadership that fosters innovation. Yet while the term is metaphorical, the phenomena it describes are quite real.

"Clockwise" is a term commonly used to describe a circular path. In this context, that path is a feedback loop. Feedback loops are a fundamental characteristic of the natural world and of all living things. Systems as large as our global weather patterns, as tiny as cellular metabolism, or as mundane as a driver steering a car are governed by feedback loops.

Our interactions with each other are also feedback loops. For example, a family, a corporation, a government, and business cycles are all composed of feedback loops. Any situation in which influence is mutual—which arguably covers all human relationships—is a feedback loop.

Feedback loops also govern the way we think and reason. The same dynamic processes that keep us alive also give us our intelligence. Clockwise Thinking is both a way of describing how those processes work and a technique for using those processes. It's not uncommon to use this technique. What is uncommon is to use it consistently and effectively, while understanding how and why it works.

There are two parts to this book. The first half explains what it means to think Clockwise—and why we so often fail to do so. It reveals easily recognized patterns that explain much of what's wrong with the way business is so often conducted and why it can be so unrewarding, even dysfunctional. Yet this first part of the book also explains techniques that anyone can use immediately to change those unproductive patterns and gain fresh insights. You could call it "practical creativity" because this approach is both highly imaginative and very pragmatic.

The second half of the book builds on those concepts to explain Innovative Leadership. Again, it reveals many destructive patterns and then explains how to change those patterns. Clockwise Thinking is effective when even just one person employs it. But its power grows exponentially when spread throughout a business or other organization. The leadership imperative is to not only use Clockwise Thinking, but to create an environment that encourages everyone to use it. That creates a dynamic system, a system that is able to harvest and implement great ideas.

FIELD NOTES:

Our intelligence is an extension of our biology.

Clockwise Thinking is the first pattern we used to learn about the world. There is now considerable research showing that as babies we used our imagination to make sense of what philosopher and psychologist William James called the "booming buzzing confusion" that babies must surely experience. We coupled our imagination with trial and error and gradually figured out that if we let go of something, it would fall to the floor. We discovered that if we wanted the ball to move, we had to push it, and then if we wanted it to stop, we had to grab it. Only years later would we learn to call those discoveries "gravity" and "inertia," but that was long after we were routinely using those insights to make sense of the world.

We conducted all sorts of complex experiments, gradually discovering things like shapes and sizes, textures and temperatures, Mommy and Daddy, happy and sad. We later learned to call that "playing".

That simple process of imagining possibilities, experimenting to see if they work, observing the result, and using those observations to imagine new possibilities forms a feedback loop that I call an *Insight Loop,* and it looks like this:

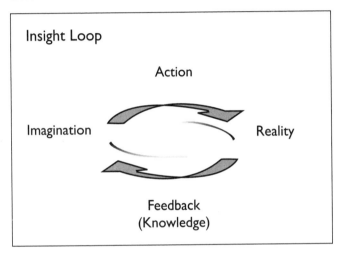

We started with imagination. It could have been any idea at all, as long as we could somehow act upon it, such as by dropping a spoon from a high chair. In other words, we tested our idea against reality. We then observed that the spoon fell to the floor, confirming our idea.

We were in effect little scientists because scientific method mimics this pattern. A scientist develops a hypothesis (imagines something), conducts an experiment (acts on that idea) to test that hypothesis, and then uses the results of that experiment (feedback) to determine whether the hypothesis was true. If the experiment confirms the hypothesis, the scientist has made a discovery, which becomes what we typically call "knowledge". If the experiment fails to confirm the original idea, the findings are used to refine the hypothesis or come up with a new one and the process is repeated.

The problem with our traditional view of knowledge is that it tends to become very static. Once we count something as knowledge, we no longer question it. It is something we consider to be "true"—it's settled.

Innovative thinking is more dynamic. It requires flexibility—which is why I prefer to call the result of such thinking "Insight" and why I call this pattern an *Insight Loop.*

Like any good scientist, and much to our parents' dismay, we confirmed our experiments many times, using a variety of objects just to be sure. As we did that, we were doing what mathematicians call "multi-variable analysis" and what computer engineers call "massive parallel processing". We were not just learning about gravity when we dropped a spoon; we were also learning about "bend over," "pick up," and "what makes Mommy or Daddy angry."

If we had been raised on a spacecraft in orbit, the weightlessness around us would have given us entirely different feedback. So we would have come to very different conclusions—but conclusions that would still have been quite accurate about our environment.

As adults, we're no longer dropping spoons to see what will happen. In a business setting, the idea we test may be a new product, a marketing plan, or a new manufacturing process. The reality we are trying to understand may be customer preferences, but the process is the same.

We generate ideas. Then we test them to see whether they work. We systematically evaluate them and use what we learn to refine our ideas and generate new ones.

It's not just using our imagination. We can have all the ideas in the world but unless we can determine that they somehow correspond to reality, they're just musings, daydreams with little practical value.

Because this system of thinking is a continuous loop, we do not always have to start with our imagination. We can choose to start at any point on the loop. We can begin with our experiences or observations or actions—as long as we keep moving in a Clockwise direction. It's the sequence that's crucial. It requires us to constantly use our imagination in a way that leads to new insights.

This pattern appears in many different activities. We see it when an entrepreneur launches a new business model, when a doctor diagnoses a patient, when a political candidate runs for elective office, or a journalist pursues a story.

We see Clockwise Thinking when a salesperson genuinely attempts to discern and solve problems for a prospect, creating a working partnership. We see it when someone provides great customer service by identifying the customer's needs and improvising a way to address them. We see it with new product development—if the tough questions get asked early and often. We see it when someone explores anything from the North Pole to a new market niche. Success in all of those endeavors and countless others requires that we discover fresh insights and this process enables us to do that.

This has always been the most efficient way to learn and discover. In our fast-paced world, it's tempting to view scientific techniques as academic, slow, and plodding—until we're reminded what the world was like before science was widely practiced. Without it, we would still be trying to turn lead into gold and treating disease with leeches.

FIELD NOTES:

Innovative thinking is not about what you know; it's about what insights you can gain.

The Knowledge Loop

When we were babies, our natural desire to discover was encouraged at first, not that we needed much encouragement to do what came so naturally. Soon however, our parents became exasperated with our experiments and began rewarding our accomplishments instead. They celebrated our first steps and first words much more than anything we learned by dropping spoons. Indeed, part of our socialization was learning that some kinds of experiments were no longer cute—or were even punishable.

As we entered school, our teachers took a similar approach. Test scores became more important than creativity. Instead of promoting our innate curiosity and sense of wonder, our teachers constantly reminded us that we were not the first to discover anything. Over time, the bulk of our education fell into a predictable sequence:

1. Someone has already figured this out for you.
2. This is the correct answer.
3. Remember it.

Without realizing it, we've been conditioned to follow a different pattern, one based not on imagination, but on knowledge, what we *know* (or, what others know that we have had to memorize). Instead of using our imagination, we've been taught to start with knowledge and go the other direction around the loop, *counterclockwise*. We've learned to literally think backwards, forming a closed feedback loop, or what I call a *Knowledge Loop*.

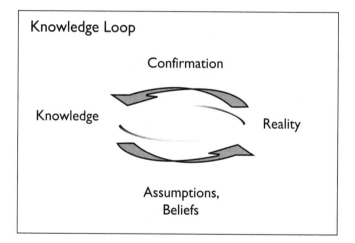

Instead of testing our ideas against reality, we've been taught to use knowledge to evaluate reality. We've learned to start with knowledge instead of imagination, and it doesn't even occur to us to think of it as feedback (partly because we weren't encouraged to discover it for ourselves in the first place). It's just what we already know. We then use knowledge to make assumptions and create beliefs. Then we use those assumptions to filter what we observe and accept as real only those things that fit with what we already believe, rejecting the rest as wrong. We reason that what we already know is "true" and what is "true" doesn't change. What then comes back to us is not new insights, but confirmation and reinforcement of what we already believe to be true.

We filter our imagination in the same way. When we have a new idea, the first thing we do is check it against what we already think we know. If the idea doesn't fit, we reject it as naïve or ignorant or stupid.

Imagination is so fundamental to the way we learn about the world that when we suppress it we develop blind spots. We miss things, sometimes things that are important and should be obvious. Psychologists have long observed a phenomenon called *selective perception*. In countless ways large and small, we fail to notice things that we don't expect. Our minds overlook things as mundane as a plate of butter on the table in front of us that we fail to pass when someone asks for it. It's right there in plain sight, but we don't see it.

In the same way, we may fail to notice things as complex as a rising competitive threat. We don't recognize the clues because we're caught in old assumptions. The problem only becomes obvious when someone later points it out, or when other symptoms (e.g. falling sales) become impossible to ignore.

Counterclockwise Thinking interferes with the successful launch of a business or the diagnosis of a medical problem because it makes assumptions instead of asking all the relevant questions. This pattern leads to the creation of political agendas rather than solutions. Reporters who think this way make the facts fit the story instead of making the story fit the facts. Companies that operate this way fail to even identify customer needs, much less meet them. Project managers following this pattern tend to delay the sort of experimentation that would identify problems early, when they are relatively cheap and easy to solve.

Most of us routinely think this way and it's absolutely toxic to innovation. Innovation requires that we develop insights and Counterclockwise Thinking does not enable us to do that. We need to overcome those long-ingrained Counterclockwise habits and get back to thinking and behaving in ways that promote learning, discovery, and innovation, rather than discouraging it. We need to think like a child again.

FIELD NOTES:

Imagination is an innate ability born into us, but we have spent most of our lives suppressing it.

Knowledge is important, but it should be treated as a source of possibilities, rather than firm conclusions and unexamined assumptions.

To fully explain the differences between Clockwise and Counterclockwise Thinking, I need to digress briefly to further explain feedback loops, and in a way that's a little different from the way they are usually defined.

A commonly used illustration of a feedback loop is the relationship between a furnace and a thermostat. When the temperature in a room drops below a certain point, the thermostat turns on the furnace, which then warms the room. When the temperature then rises to a certain point, the thermostat turns off the furnace. The temperature gradually falls and the cycle repeats. This is typically referred to as a "negative" or "closed" feedback loop because the effect is to stop the temperature from rising or falling outside a narrow range. The system "contains" the temperature.

Another common illustration of feedback is the audio feedback that occurs in a public address system when someone puts a microphone too close to one of the loudspeakers. The amplified sound coming out of the speaker is picked up by the microphone, fed back into the system, and re-amplified. So, it comes out of the speaker still louder. It's picked up again by the microphone and amplified again. The result is a shrill tone at maximum volume. This is referred to as a "positive" or "open" feedback loop because it amplifies the sound, making it louder and louder—limited only by how much energy is available to the system.

That's where these illustrations normally stop, but I want to expand and refine them a little in order to better characterize what is really happening. I want to separate the concepts of *feedback* and *feedback loops*. To avoid confusion, I will continue to refer to feedback as positive and negative, and refer to feedback loops as open and closed.

As a furnace turns on and off, it's actually providing both negative and positive feedback. The feedback is positive when it's on and warms the room and negative when it's off and allows the room to cool. The thermostat is also providing both types of feedback—positive when it turns the furnace on, negative when it turns it off. So what is occurring is both positive and negative feedback within a closed feedback loop.

With the public address system, the feedback is positive because it amplifies the sound, but that feedback loop is also closed. Like the furnace and thermostat, the microphone and speaker are part of a self-contained system operating more or less mechanically.

Noise cancellation technology is the negative equivalent of audio feedback. With noise cancellation, the sound waves coming through the microphone are inverted electronically and fed into the same circuit. The inverted wave cancels the original wave, creating silence. That is negative feedback within a closed feedback loop.

Under these refined definitions, mechanical systems are invariably closed feedback loops. They are designed to create a predetermined outcome. Open feedback loops are those things that grow and evolve. That includes the natural world around us and things like businesses and economies.

(Another way to distinguish between the two is to say that closed feedback loops are those that can be characterized with traditional linear mathematics, and open feedback loops are those represented by non-linear mathematics. Non-linear math models the way crystals develop or a nautilus shell grows. These are referred to as "fractals" in chaos and complexity theory. However, that is beyond the scope of this book.)

For now, it's sufficient to understand that positive feedback and open feedback loops are what make living organisms grow and thunderstorms build. Negative feedback and closed feedback loops keep us from growing 20 feet tall. A successful business is the result of positive feedback. Money is invested that generates profits, which allow for increased investment, which leads to higher profits. If that feedback turns negative, then the business becomes unprofitable and will eventually fail.

Businesses must maintain positive feedback in order to grow and prosper. However, it is possible for a business to grow too fast. To be successful, a business must use both open and closed feedback loops, to promote and guide healthy growth.

Stock markets display the interplay of positive and negative feedback on a massive scale. Some feedback promotes higher prices and growth, while other feedback tends to dampen them. Which one is most dominant determines whether it's a bear or a bull market. Yet even the complexity of a stock market is 2 + 2 compared to the natural world around us, which is a massive web of feedback loops.

Our bodies utilize both positive and negative feedback and both open and closed feedback loops to regulate everything from our appetite to our body temperature, from our respiration to our perspiration.

Needless to say, feedback loops can be incredibly powerful forces. Clockwise Thinking harnesses those forces.

A Feedback Matrix

When we interact with the world, we get both positive and negative feedback. In other words, we succeed or we fail. That feedback is inescapable, no matter how we think, but the way we process "success" or "failure" when we think Clockwise is radically different from the way we process it when we think Counterclockwise.

When we think Clockwise following an Insight Loop, positive feedback is a discovery. The data confirm what we imagined, so we have learned something new. Negative feedback fails to confirm our ideas, but we can use that data to refine our ideas and generate new ones. So, learning still results. Either outcome is beneficial: heads we win and tails we win.

When we think Counterclockwise, following a Knowledge Loop, positive feedback is confirmation but it is not a discovery because it's not confirming anything new. Negative feedback is failure, period. We only learn what does not work (and may not even grasp that). We haven't created any new solutions because we haven't attempted anything beyond what we already thought we knew. These relationships are illustrated by a matrix:

FEEDBACK	Negative (Failure)	Positive (Success)
Counterclockwise (Closed Loop)	Failure	Confirmation
Clockwise (Open Loop)	Learning	Discovery

When *Counterclockwise Thinking* encounters *negative* feedback, the result is *failure*.

When *Counterclockwise Thinking* encounters *positive* feedback, the result is *confirmation* but there is no new information.

When *Clockwise Thinking* encounters *negative* feedback, something is *learned*.

When *Clockwise Thinking* encounters *positive* feedback, it confirms a new idea so something is *discovered*.

With *Counterclockwise Thinking*, no outcomes lead to fresh insights. With *Clockwise Thinking*, all possible outcomes contribute to fresh insights.

FIELD NOTES:

Thinking Clockwise, like innovation and creativity, is an iterative process. Each lap around the loop affects the next one in a constantly evolving pattern.

Two Ways of Thinking

Obviously, Clockwise and Counterclockwise Thinking are radically different ways of approaching the world. Both form feedback loops, but Counterclockwise is closed and therefore limited and confining. It leads to conformity and reinforces the status quo. Clockwise is an open loop and therefore expansive and creative. It remains constantly open to new possibilities. Counterclockwise reduces the number of possible solutions while Clockwise increases them. Counterclockwise is slow to adapt while Clockwise can adapt quickly.

When viewed from a Counterclockwise perspective, Clockwise Thinking may appear naïve and undisciplined, but it is brutally pragmatic. It forces us to make our thoughts and actions correspond to reality. It continually questions assumptions to be sure that nothing has been overlooked or taken for granted. Counterclockwise Thinking often relies on long-held beliefs, whether they correspond to reality or not.

All of us have been immersed in Counterclockwise Thinking throughout our lives. Like the mythical boy raised by wolves—who came to believe he was a wolf—we are very comfortable thinking that way.

Just as we can constantly think Counterclockwise, there is no reason why we can't constantly think Clockwise, if we choose to. It takes a conscious and concerted effort to reverse those patterns. Yet when we do, we unleash our creativity and gain new insights. We employ the most powerful intellectual tool ever devised—the one we were born with.

Both Clockwise and Counterclockwise Thinking are coherent ways to look at the world. It is possible to function using either approach, but each implies different values and leads to different actions.

Clockwise Thinking embodies the values most of us embrace, while Counterclockwise Thinking tends to undermine those values. That contrast is one of the most compelling arguments that can be made in support of Clockwise Thinking.

When we think Clockwise, we value:

Faith and Courage

Clockwise Thinking requires courage, a willingness to take risks. We must act on our ideas in order to determine their validity, so we must muster the faith and courage to face uncertainty.

Goals

Setting hoped-for outcomes is essential to Clockwise Thinking. We have to determine in advance what will count as success. Otherwise, we have no way of determining whether we have been effective or ineffective at the end of the day. If we can't answer that simple question, we have no way to evaluate the feedback and we stop moving around the loop. Without goals, the process stalls. We need some benchmark to measure the success or effectiveness of our actions—without prescribing those actions.

Humility

In order to avoid falling into Counterclockwise assumptions, we must constantly recognize that our ideas are subject to re-evaluation. We need to maintain a sense of humility about our thoughts and actions. In the real world, each situation is unique. So the outcome is uncertain no matter how much knowledge we have.

FIELD NOTES:

With Clockwise Thinking, courage and humility are not competing values that must be balanced. They reinforce each other. When we think this way, we do not have to choose between the humble demeanor of the monk and the supreme confidence of the fighter pilot; we become both.

Integrity

Integrity is critical if we're going to gain insight by observing the feedback that inevitably follows our actions. If we are not striving to be honest—especially with ourselves—then we're corrupting the data.

FIELD NOTES:

In theory, this is the proper role of accountants and journalists, to provide reliable data so that valid inferences can be drawn from that feedback.

Education

Education is important, not so much because it teaches us facts about the world, but because it teaches us how to reason through various possibilities. The world is a dangerous place. Some experiments are too risky or expensive to conduct. So we need to model possibilities and learn from other people's experiences. We use our ability to reason not to simply memorize what other people have learned, but to run experiments in our head. Then we don't need to touch every stove to see whether it's hot.

This is different from Counterclockwise education, which focuses on learning the right answers and drawing conclusions. Drawing firm conclusions is the surest way to stop gaining new insights.

FIELD NOTES:

If all the inventors who attempted to build the airplane had flown their first designs off a hundred-foot cliff, the rest of us would still be taking the train.

Communication

Clockwise Thinking believes the more ideas the better. We need to learn from each other's experiences, sharing lessons learned and insights gained. That requires robust communication and interactions.

Pragmatism

"Does it *work*?" is the key question. The emphasis is on solving problems and making things happen. Successfully applying an idea in the real world is ultimately the only definitive test of its validity.

FIELD NOTES:

Success is a product of skill and insight. Knowledge is necessary; it's just not enough.

Counterclockwise Thinking embodies values that may at first appear benign or even admirable, but they can play out in less than ideal ways. They reflect a way of thinking that tends to become rigid, tradition bound, and ideological.

When we think Counterclockwise, we value:

Stability

When we base our success on what we already know, the last thing we want to contend with is new circumstances. Anything that undermines the validity of existing knowledge is a threat. So we resist change.

Execution

In a stable environment where no adaptation is required, the fastest, strongest, and smartest will prevail. It's about execution. The objective is to be as good as possible at what we already know how to do. Unfortunately, our environment is rarely stable so we need to be able to adapt.

Clockwise Thinking is about effective execution, too, but in ways that allow for ongoing adjustments and improvements.

Elimination of Risk

The goal is to play it safe and eliminate all risk, so that we can execute as flawlessly as possible.

FIELD NOTES:

Life is inherently risky, so trying to be completely safe is futile. Safety is important, but too much emphasis on safety is paralyzing because it reduces our ability to adapt. Instead of making us safer, that overemphasis makes us more vulnerable.

Persistence

When we believe we already know what to do, the only seeming obstacle to our success is failing to try hard enough. We think we just need to keep doing more of the same until it works.

FIELD NOTES:

Albert Einstein famously defined insanity as doing the same thing over and over again and expecting different results.

Conformity

If we already know the best way to do things, then any deviation is counterproductive. Creative ideas are unnecessary fluff—or even a threat. The goal of education—or corporate training—tends to become indoctrination.

Certainty

When our success is based on knowledge, we think our goal should be to know as much as possible, as firmly as possible.

Counterclockwise Thinking is something we all do. It's a habit that is so ingrained in us that we have all but lost our awareness of it. We notice it no more than we notice our breathing.

As I have already noted, Counterclockwise Thinking is a closed feedback loop. Much of what we call "culture" is a system of closed feedback loops that we have invented to manage ourselves. They consist of such things as our cultural mores, our values and rules of morality, our legal and criminal justice systems, and so forth. Those things are essential to any functioning society, so we teach them to our children. We do our best to get our children to internalize them and teach them to their children.

Unfortunately, as we do that, we teach our children to *think* that way. *Counterclockwise Thinking* is not necessary to a functioning society, but we have long assumed that it is, because we have not realized that there is any alternative.

We have long sensed that there is a problem with the way we think. So we urge people to be more "flexible" and "open minded". But that is sometimes perceived as threatening to social norms—because we confuse the need for appropriate social boundaries with the way we think and reason. As a result, progress seems to require that we not only adopt new ideas; it requires rejecting old ones that we have been taught are true. Our natural tendency is to resist because we see those new ideas as the wrong answers. We reason that what was true yesterday cannnot suddenly become untrue today.

Counterclockwise Thinking has created an intellectual morass we have to slog through to get anywhere. It's the primary reason that change is often such a protracted and painful process, why it encounters so much seemingly irrational resistance.

FIELD NOTES:

Counterclockwise Thinking is often easier to recognize in others than in ourselves.

○ We're Thinking Counterclockwise When . . .

We Resist Change

When we believe we already have command of the truth, change becomes a huge emotional hurdle. It seems like it requires rejecting the truth. Rather than seeing a reward in inventing new approaches, we see it as upsetting or perhaps as an assault on our values. Change is often just a hassle we would rather avoid.

We get so invested in what we know that we are only willing to add to the list, not rethink any of our assumptions. We like things to be predictable and settled, which of course life isn't, so we try to maintain control wherever we can.

When we move Counterclockwise from reality to imagination, we're limiting our ideas to what we can already see.

When we see ourselves as successful, Counterclockwise patterns reinforce our convictions and make us overly skeptical of new ideas. When we are unsure of ourselves, those same patterns lead us to cling to whatever information and skills we feel we have.

FIELD NOTES:

This is what we commonly call, "Staying in our comfort zone."

↻ We're Thinking Counterclockwise When . . .

We're Overconfident

We believe what worked in the past is a sufficient test for what will work in the present and in the future. That's because what worked then is based on what we already think we know to be true and that does not change. So, when things are going well, we tend to dismiss any doubts or reservations. Our attitude is that it's "good enough". So we don't strive for improvements or investigate potential flaws.

When we think this way, "better" may mean faster, cheaper, or more efficient, but it does not mean "significantly different".

FIELD NOTES:

The surest way to stop learning is to conclude that we already have all the answers.

↺ We're Thinking Counterclockwise When . . .

We Over-Generalize

We apply a finite set of explanations in many different contexts without considering the subtleties of each situation. This is the "one-size-fits-all" approach to problem solving.

People who take this approach have blind spots, areas where they fail to recognize that they are missing important things about a situation. Not only do their solutions often fail, they may not even recognize those failures, much less learn from them so they can devise better solutions. Instead they tend to force the data to fit their preconceived ideas.

This is moving Counterclockwise along the bottom of the feedback loop, from knowledge to reality. It is starting with what we already believe and insisting that reality fit it.

This is not the same as having core values. Core values can still be adapted to fit a variety of circumstances. The problem comes when those values become so rigid that they no longer work well in some situations, when they're applied arbitrarily without carefully evaluating their impact. This happens when we're no longer willing to ask ourselves the tough questions, when relevant feedback is ignored or dismissed.

FIELD NOTES:

Dogs do this when they chase cars. If it's moving, they mindlessly go after it. Sometimes we need to pause and ask ourselves, "How many cars am I chasing?"

↺ We're Thinking Counterclockwise When . . .

We Place Blame

When we think we already know how things work, we tend to view cause and effect relationships as a matter of mechanics. So we address problems by looking for where things broke down, wondering, "Who did something wrong?" Our goal then is to restore the status quo.

When someone's explanation points to systemic problems rather than personal mistakes, we view it as an excuse. Our focus is on keeping the "machinery" running smoothly rather than on changing the system. So we don't seek novel solutions or improvements.

Moving Counterclockwise around the loop means looking for solutions by reviewing what we already know to be true.

In the real world, it is rarely as simple as A leads to B leads to C because B and C often influence A and each other. Changing the product may change customer behavior. Changing prices usually changes demand. Changes in marketing strategy may prompt changes by competitors. Dismissing an employee may affect the productivity of his or her former colleagues.

In complex systems cause and effect are not always clear and such systems tend to break down in complex ways. The solution is not always as simple as fixing a leaking hose or a broken gasket—or correcting someone's "mistake".

⟳ We're Thinking Counterclockwise When . . .

We Prefer Certainty to Curiosity

It becomes very important to us to have the right answer. So we ask few questions. We have been taught all our lives that the goal is to know stuff and how much stuff we know defines how smart we are. So we have an emotional aversion to admitting that we don't know something.

When we focus too much on what we "know," we lack interest in new ideas and perspectives, preferring instead to stay with what is already familiar.

When we think Counterclockwise, failure has no value. So we avoid taking risks.

When we encounter a new idea, rather than evaluate it on its merits (which might require some detailed investigation), we tend to evaluate it based on the beliefs we already have about the source. This phenomenon can manifest itself in at least three ways:

1. We latch onto ideas that appeal to us without much skepticism. If we like the source (including ourselves), we like the idea. If the source mirrors our own race, culture, gender, or political party preference, we feel more comfortable with ideas from that source. If the source is someone who we already believe to be a competent expert, then we embrace the idea. We may then implement those ideas without enough thought, research, or preparation.

2. We dismiss ideas too quickly when we don't judge the source as being credible. So we miss many viable options.

3. We tend to blur the distinction between facts and opinions. When we find the source credible, we treat opinion as though it's fact. When we don't find the source credible, we treat facts as just opinions.

FIELD NOTES:

An example of this need to always be right isthe proverbial male trait of being unwilling to ask for directions

↺ We're Thinking Counterclockwise When . . .

We Over-Emphasize Rules

We think there is a right way and a wrong way to do things, so we tend to ignore other options. We believe that keeping things consistent for everyone assures fairness, so we resist anything that varies from current norms. We believe rules are there to prescribe the way things should be done, period. When someone figures out a way to do things differently—even within existing rules—we tend to view that as trying to beat the system. So our inclination is to tighten the rules.

When we are focused on rules, we expect someone to ask permission before making changes, and when we are in charge, our inclination is not to grant permission without a compelling reason. Our paramount goal is to maintain order and predictability. The fact that these attitudes are absolutely toxic to innovation and creativity—and therefore progress—has probably never occurred to us.

There are of course times when enforcing the rules is appropriate. Certainly that is true for a police officer, a judge, or a prosecutor. But it is also important to note that our criminal justice system is based primarily on setting boundaries and if something is not explicitly prohibited, it's allowed.

FIELD NOTES:

The principle, "If it's not prohibited, it's allowed," is embodied in the U.S. Constitution. It was included so that the government could never change the rules to make something illegal after the fact. Article 1, Section 9. "No bill of attainder or ex post facto law shall be passed."

↺ We're Thinking Counterclockwise When . . .

We Ignore Feedback

We become so focused on doing what we already know how to do that we fail to notice when our actions become less effective. We view failure as a flaw, so we avoid it whenever possible and deny or minimize it when it occurs.

As a result, we do not learn from our mistakes. We may focus on improving our skills to better execute a task, but we don't consider whether the task should be changed or whether it should even be executed.

Because we fail to appreciate the value of feedback, we see little value in experimentation. So we become risk averse. We become so determined to avoid failure that we refuse to experiment at all. Or we may seek to test things only in ways that will confirm what we already believe. So we have no way to evaluate new possibilities accurately.

FIELD NOTES:

We all know people who won't accept feedback. You just can't tell them anything. They think they already know it all. It's the "13-year-old syndrome".

↺ We're Thinking Counterclockwise When . . .

We Have a Low Tolerance for Differing Opinions

As we strive to accumulate knowledge, we have little interest in hearing anything that contradicts those things that we have already concluded to be true. Changing our minds requires a compelling argument, and it must be rooted in our assumptions. We quickly lose patience with those who don't share our values. They're simply "wrong", or they "just don't get it."

We are not particularly interested in finding common ground with those who disagree with us, because we see no need to reconsider our perspective. To us, they're obviously the ones who need to change. When they won't do that, it doesn't make sense to us. So we become suspicious of their motives, or question their intelligence. It tends to make us angry.

Holding onto and defending our opinions becomes a point of pride and personal power. Conceding that someone else has won an argument is an unacceptable humiliation.

One of the surest indicators of Counterclockwise Thinking is becoming agitated or angry over someone's differing point of view. That emotional response reveals that we have locked onto our own perspective. We are treating what we believe to be true not as a source of possibilities, but of firm conclusions.

> FIELD NOTES:
>
> Think of your last political discussion.

⟲ We're Thinking Counterclockwise When ...

We Develop Blind Spots

This is one of the most dangerous things about Counterclockwise Thinking. It does not just fail to promote discovery and innovation; it blinds us to the problems around us.

This is what investigators concluded caused the tragic breakup of the Space Shuttle Columbia and the earlier loss of the Space Shuttle Challenger.

The report released by the Columbia Accident Investigation Board concluded: The foam did it. A piece of insulating foam that struck the left wing on liftoff, breaking a hole in the heat shielding, led to the disaster on re-entry, 16 days later. But more importantly, the report noted that:

"A high-risk rescue mission might have been mounted…if management had recognized the severity of the problem and acted quickly."

"The problem that doomed Columbia and its crew—even after liftoff—was not a lack of technology or ability, but missed opportunities and a lack of leadership and open-mindedness…"

Dr. Sally Ride, the first American woman in space and a member of the investigating board, believes that the Columbia tragedy and the 1986 Challenger Space Shuttle disaster resulted from the same mindset, saying,

"(NASA) managers…did not grab onto this problem and insist on an answer. It was really quite the opposite. They assumed they knew the answer. They assumed the foam was not going to be a problem. And they were insisting that people disprove the preconception they had."

NASA is arguably the most brilliant scientific organization in the world, but it failed because some very bright, competent, committed people stopped thinking scientifically. It's not about how smart we are or how much we care; it's about the patterns we follow. The problem with relying too much on existing knowledge and expertise is that in a complex system, everything is changing. There are always new problems, new variables, new challenges.

Few of us will ever have to get a space shuttle into orbit and back safely. But a business is a complex system. The world is a complex system. We all spend our lives navigating our way through complex systems. When we approach those challenges with closed loop Counterclockwise Thinking, we're courting disaster.

FIELD NOTES:

Science is the ultimate in Clockwise Thinking but scientists are also some of the worst offenders. In every field of science each successive paradigm tends to become the reigning Counterclockwise dogma, until someone breaks that pattern with a fresh Clockwise approach.

Generally speaking, Clockwise Thinking is what the metaphor implies. It's moving forward, progressing, advancing, and being productive. Counterclockwise Thinking is counterproductive. It slows progress or even reverses it. We all commonly practice and observe both behaviors, both ways of thinking.

Because they're feedback loops, both ways of thinking are self-reinforcing patterns or habits. Left undisturbed, Counterclockwise Thinking will continue. Yet if allowed to, Clockwise Thinking will grow and evolve of its own accord. Simply recognizing the pattern and believing it has value tends to promote it.

There are a number of things that characterize Clockwise Thinking and distinguish it from Counterclockwise Thinking. Clockwise Thinking provides all the intellectual tools we need to function effectively, without the problems that Counterclockwise Thinking creates.

○ We're Thinking Clockwise When . . .

We Consider Multiple Options

Clockwise Thinking means that when faced with a problem, we do not default to the way it's been handled before, or go with the first solution that occurs to us. It means recognizing that there is always more than one possible solution. So we consider a range of possibilities, based on our own ideas and those of others.

This is the imagination part of the feedback loop. We start with what we believe to be true, but we don't stop there. Past experiences and practices are important, but they do not automatically override other possibilities.

FIELD NOTES:

It is often those people who are most competent who fail to see the alternatives. They already know of at least one solution, or can easily invent one. So they choose a solution too quickly and miss opportunities to improve.

⟲ We're Thinking Clockwise When . . .

We Make Connections

As we seek options, we look for connections. Clockwise Thinking takes the available information and resources and seeks to recombine them in novel ways. This is the essence of creativity. It is rarely if ever the proverbial "bolt out of the blue," but rather something built of pre-existing pieces.

Imagination is fundamental to our thinking, so any of us can use it. It's not a matter of learning how to imagine, so much as releasing that potential. When we think this way, we may use a variety of techniques: brainstorming, daydreaming, ideation, thinking out loud, or just playing, to release our own innate creativity. Such techniques are really strategies to "get our head turned around," to break out of ingrained Counterclockwise habits.

FIELD NOTES:

When we are being creative, the objective is not knowledge and certainty, but rather fresh insights.

○ We're Thinking Clockwise When . . .

We're Curious

When we're always probing and asking questions like, "How?" and, "Why?" we are not just seeking to master a set of skills, but to gain new information. Moving Clockwise around the loop means we are constantly open to new ideas. It's wanting answers, but always having more questions, always evaluating and reevaluating possibilities.

We are using our imagination to formulate possible answers that we can investigate and either confirm or disprove.

FIELD NOTES:

This is what a good journalist does. Reporting is not passive observation. It is an active creative process of seeking to discover interesting facts and scenarios that make a good story.

⟲ We're Thinking Clockwise When . . .

We Challenge Assumptions

We're doing this when we are careful to always acknowledge what we do not know. We strive to be alert to subtle distinctions and to recognize both our assumptions and those of others. We need to understand that in the real world our actions are inherently experimental. They always include some degree of uncertainty.

To avoid hidden assumptions, it is important to keep track of where we are on the Insight Loop. When we are on the top of the loop, we are acting on our ideas and opinions and they need to be tested. When we are on the bottom of the loop, we are receiving and interpreting feedback and we need to evaluate that data carefully. We have to make some assumptions in order to function, but it is important to treat them as assumptions, not conclusions.

FIELD NOTES:

Facts should be treated very differently from ideas. The reliability of facts and data is dependent on the credibility of the source and the integrity we apply when we interpret that data. The value of an idea is intrinsic to the idea; its source is irrelevant.

○ We're Thinking Clockwise When . . .

We Model Possibilities

The question we should seek to answer is a very practical one: "What works?" Yet it is not practical to turn everything into an experiment. Most of us consider it a safe bet that the sun will come up in the morning and we don't lose any sleep trying to test that. (Although having scientists scan the sky for errant asteroids heading our way may seem like a good idea.)

Rather than test every idea with an experiment, we use our ability to reason to develop mental models of possibilities. This is different from Counterclockwise Thinking, because we are not just applying our knowledge. We're recognizing that every situation is unique. So existing knowledge may or may not be a good predictor of a particular outcome. Modeling is how we use our intellect to apply both knowledge and imagination to each new situation.

FIELD NOTES:

Recalling facts and repeating past practices is not really reasoning. Reasoning through something is the process of mentally modeling a scenario.

(U) We're Thinking Clockwise When . . .

We Think in Terms of Outcomes

It is crucial that we have defined objectives. When a scientist conducts an experiment, there is always an expected result. Otherwise, there is no way to determine whether the experiment is a success or a failure and nothing is learned. Outcomes provide the criteria we need to evaluate the feedback that will inevitably follow, so we can learn from the experience.

Clockwise Thinking sets outcomes to clarify what needs to be achieved, without predetermining exactly what means may be needed to achieve it.

This is the opposite of ideology. An ideology assumes that if certain steps are taken, a specific outcome will inevitably follow. Clockwise Thinking turns that around, recognizing that getting to a desired outcome may require different approaches under different circumstances.

Reversing Cause and Effect

One of the characteristics of a feedback loop is that cause and effect flow both ways. It seems counterintuitive that an outcome can be the cause of something, but that is exactly how we make decisions.

Counterclockwise Thinking views the world mechanically. In the social sciences that view is called Determinism, the theory that human behavior is the result of a complex sequence of causes dating back to our birth and beyond. It is the belief that we do what we do because we are driven to do it.

A Determinist would argue that someone who invests in the stock market is compelled to do that by his or her disposition and upbringing. Perhaps the person had parents who instilled a strong sense of thrift and taught him or her the skills of money management.

Clockwise Thinking makes the outcome the cause. It is the belief that someone invests in the stock market for a much simpler reason: They want to make money.

That's an outcome.

We use the same approach to make all of the important decisions of our lives. When we decide where to live, what career to pursue, whom to make a life with, whether to have children, even what route to travel to work in the morning, we are deciding based on expected or intended or hoped for outcomes.

Failing to think in terms of outcomes is irrational. It is acting merely on impulse. If you're so compelled by your upbringing that you would invest in the stock market even when you expected it to lose your money, then I'm sorry, but you need professional help (financial and otherwise)!

When we think in terms of desired outcomes, we are following the same feedback patterns that give us life.

FIELD NOTES:

The only rational cause is an outcome.

Goals are tools.

⟳ We're Thinking Clockwise When ...

We Experiment

We must constantly experiment. Life is inescapably uncertain and risky. We can never have all the relevant information or complete certainty about any outcome. So we give it our best. We choose a course of action and we act. That is ultimately the only way to test our ideas and only by testing ideas can we gain new insights.

This is the step that must follow imagination in Clockwise Thinking, taking us across the top of the *Insight Loop*. Even inaction is a decision, and it will bring some outcome. So we might as well make it into an experiment so we can evaluate the results and learn from the experience.

To truly experiment, we must define not only what will count as success, but exactly what will tell us when we've failed. If we are not willing to acknowledge failure, then we are not experimenting. We're just confirming our opinions.

FIELD NOTES:

Life is an experiment.

⟳ We're Thinking Clockwise When …

We Welcome a Challenge

In life, failure is part of the package. We need courage to take the risks necessary to test our ideas. We need to recognize that failure is also a source of insight that leads ultimately to success—as long as we learn from our mistakes. We need to master the paradox of acting with conviction while humbly acknowledging that we may be wrong.

Clockwise Thinking means we are comfortable with uncertainty and ambiguity. It means working hard to achieve successful outcomes while thriving on solving problems along the way.

↺ We're Thinking Clockwise When ...

We Analyze the Results of Our Actions

We take time to reflect on our actions and ask ourselves whether the outcome is what we expected. Then we ask, "Why or why not?" Rather then seeking certainty, we strive to accumulate ever-improving insights that we use to refine our imagination and guide our actions. We continually monitor our actions and note the feedback. Then we make adjustments and course corrections as early as possible to keep moving efficiently toward our goals.

This is the bottom side of an *Insight Loop* and it is a crucial link. Without it, we gain no insight.

Reality is constantly providing us with feedback, but unless we're thinking Clockwise, we are not receiving all of it. When we think Counterclockwise, we only notice those things that fit what we already believe to be true.

FIELD NOTES:

All we ever really know for sure is what worked or didn't work last time (and even that's subject to interpretation).

○ We're Thinking Clockwise When ...

We Enjoy a Sense of Discovery

When we are more concerned about being successful than being right; when we appreciate a great insight
whether it's ours or someone else's; when we know how
to be completely invested in the process of thinking and
learning and innovating, without being too personally
invested in any specific outcome—then we're thinking
Clockwise.

Success is something to be celebrated, but so is the
discovery of new insights—including the ones that result
from failure. When our success confirms an idea, that is
truly a "Eureka!" moment.

FIELD NOTES:

*Everything anyone ever created or achieved required
insights. The key is in knowing how to find them.*

◡ We're Thinking Clockwise When . . .

We Keep Moving Around the Loop

Clockwise Thinking is what mathematicians call an *iterative process*. It's a formula that we need to repeat over and over again. With each attempt we get a little closer to the truth. It's a process of applying imagination, setting objectives, then acting to achieve those objectives. That creates feedback, which we analyze to gain insights. We then use those insights to refine our imagination and repeat.

We can also keep moving around the loop Counterclockwise—and often do. But when we go in that direction, there is no iteration. Because it's a closed feedback loop, it only generates repetition. It only creates more of the same, not new ideas or approaches.

It does not necessarily matter where we begin the loop. Imagination is a crucial component, but we don't always have to start there. We may start with the facts available to us or with what we observe, or with what has been done before. We may start by acting on certain beliefs and assumptions, much like Counterclockwise Thinking, but we go in the other direction. The important thing is that we move Clockwise around the loop.

The most challenging part of Clockwise Thinking isn't drawing on our imagination. We were born to do that. The really hard part is analyzing the feedback, something Counterclockwise Thinking does not even attempt. A scientist seeks to study a single variable at a time, or a limited number of them. In that way a specific cause and effect relationship can be isolated and confusion is kept to a minimum. However, in the real world, our actions change many things at once.

It may take a series of actions and careful thought to discern all the relevant relationships. Even then, the answers are rarely if ever definitive. Both Clockwise and Counterclockwise Thinking are inherently tentative, but Counterclockwise Thinking pretends to achieve certainty. The advantage of Clockwise Thinking is that it recognizes the limits of knowledge and strives to account for them.

FIELD NOTES:

In the real world, all our knowledge is inherently tentative.

↻ We're Thinking Clockwise When . . .

We Assume Responsibility

Clockwise Thinking is empowering because it provides the ability to invent new approaches. Any one of us can do this and therefore we all have a responsibility to. Instead of only looking for ways to fix what's broken or correct someone's mistakes, we are free to find the best way to do something, whatever that might be. Our own creativity becomes our primary source of solutions.

When we fail (as we surely will at times) we don't look for someone to blame for our failure; we take it as valuable feedback from which we can learn and we try again.

Clockwise Thinking drives a sense of personal and collective responsibility, the belief that the solutions we need are out there and we can find them.

Part Two: Innovative Leadership

Building an Innovation Engine

Open feedback loops are sometimes called amplifying feedback. One of the most dramatic examples of an open feedback loop is an explosion. As each molecule ignites, it releases energy, which ignites other molecules. However, the result is much more powerful than a simple domino effect or chain reaction because those individual events interact. Each tiny ignition mutually reinforces and amplifies another. The hot gases released by each molecule heat the gases released by surrounding molecules, and are heated by the gases that those other molecules release. The total effect is dramatically greater than the sum of the parts.

The result is a massive burst of energy with tremendous destructive force and sometimes tragic consequences—unless it occurs inside an engine. The engine of a car, truck, or train is a carefully designed system of closed feedback loops that contain gasoline or diesel explosions, harness them, and use them to perform productive work. Jet engines and rocket engines utilize the same principles.

Those engines do not extinguish or prevent explosions. On the contrary, they are designed to create explosions. Without them, the engine could not function. The bigger the explosions, the more powerful the engine, as long as the engine is strong enough to contain them.

Every business or organization needs some closed feedback loops in order to function. Things like management structures, accounting procedures, job descriptions, pay scales, and legal and ethical boundaries function as the pistons, valves, and crankshaft of the engine, but they are not what drive it. They are not what give it energy. That comes from the explosions—of ideas and creativity and motivation and purpose—that are embodied in the mission of the organization and the people who are part of it. It doesn't matter whether that mission is to build widgets, provide services, or help the homeless. Every organization needs those explosions.

The remainder of this book is about how to ignite robust explosions and efficiently harness them. It's about how to create and maintain an organization that learns and adapts and evolves, one that maintains a culture of innovation and creative problem solving.

It's about building an innovation engine.

Such an engine is a unique sort of machine. Like the human body or any other living organism, it is a machine based not just on mechanics, but on dynamic interactions and feedback. Yet even the human body is less dynamic than this sort of engine because an innovation engine evolves like an entire natural system. It has the ability to grow and adapt and reshape itself.

Innovation Environment

Allow me to go back to the life sciences for a moment. No living organism can exist independent of its environment. If the earth was not flooded with sunlight, there would be no plants. If we were not immersed in an ocean of air that contains oxygen, we wouldn't be here and neither would any other animal. There are all sorts of necessary interconnections between a plant or animal and its surroundings, and those interconnections form complex systems of feedback loops.

Ideas behave in much the same way. They need the right kind of environment in order to live and grow. A well-formed idea, like a seed, contains the essential information it needs to grow into something of value—if put into the right context, it will mature and thrive. Without the right environment, promising ideas will die just as surely as a plant will die without enough nourishing soil, water, and sunlight.

Maintaining Clockwise Thinking within an organization requires creating and maintaining a healthy idea-friendly environment. Just as Clockwise and Counter-clockwise Thinking each have certain attributes, so does the environment. Some of those characteristics are healthy for Clockwise Thinking while others are toxic.

Values

Toxic: The organization's values are unclear, inconsistent, or even contradictory. They reflect Counterclockwise Thinking, so new ideas are met with skepticism or outright hostility. Management's actions are not consistent with its pronouncements. There is a general attitude of, "Keep your head down," and, "Do your own job." Management and employees have different agendas and expectations. There is little trust.

Healthy: Values are broadly articulated and agreed upon throughout the organization and they provide a sense of unity. The values reflect Clockwise Thinking and include respect for differing opinions and support for a variety of ideas—whatever the source. Questions are welcomed. Creativity is encouraged and rewarded. So are openness, communication, and collaboration so that creative connections can readily occur.

The organization is willing to take risks and recognizes that risk-taking requires courage and a tolerance for failures. Management understands that integrity at all levels is crucial to getting accurate feedback to guide business decisions. Thanks to that integrity, there is strong mutual trust.

> FIELD NOTES:
>
> Values cannot be imposed, so the goal should be to embrace and accommodate values as broadly as possible.

Mission

Toxic: The mission is unclear or nonexistent. It may have been created with broad input, or by an elite group of executives, but it has become irrelevant or untouchable or both. As circumstances have evolved, it has lost its value as a guide and is not well understood by those who are responsible for implementing it. So people do not know how they can contribute. With no agreed upon criteria for judging the value of ideas, most are either ignored or implemented for the wrong reasons.

Healthy: The organization's mission is clearly articulated and well understood. It is designed to be flexible and is subject to review and revision as circumstances change. That keeps it relevant to the immediate tasks at hand. It also provides criteria that can be used to evaluate new ideas and measure their success.

A clear mission also gives meaning to everyone's work. It's what makes that work rewarding and provides a sense of fulfillment.

FIELD NOTES:

A well-defined mission is an essential tool that everyone in the organization must have.

Policies

Toxic: Policies are prescriptive. Job descriptions are very specific and allow for little discretion. The mantra is, "Ask first," so decisions tend to get pushed up the chain of command. Each administrative layer strives to avoid responsibility for any deviations because change is treated as something that should be minimized whenever possible. Mistakes are not tolerated.

Whenever there is a problem, management typically creates a new policy to address it and applies that policy throughout the company. The goal is to keep things simple by demanding conformity. Failures are penalized.

Healthy: Policies are designed to set clear legal, ethical, and operational boundaries yet grant discretion wherever possible. Within those boundaries thoughtful experimentation is allowed and encouraged. Job descriptions set responsibilities without prescribing exactly how those responsibilities must always be met. People are urged to develop personal decision-making competencies. When mistakes are made, the solution is usually coaching rather than discipline.

Whenever restrictions are necessary, they are carefully targeted to address the problem with minimal impact on anyone or anything else. Failure is acceptable within the context of thoughtful experiments, so it becomes a source for new learning and for the next thoughtful experiment.

FIELD NOTES:

underlying assumption· If it's not prohibited, it's allowed.

Communications

Toxic: Information is provided on a need-to-know basis. Managers tend to act as gatekeepers or buffers to restrict information flow. Power is focused in nodes around those who jealously guard their prerogatives, creating information bottlenecks. Any talk about problems is generally seen as unwelcome complaining. Ideas are evaluated based on their source and those with less status are discouraged from offering any ideas at all. Rumors are a constant distraction and source of misinformation.

Healthy: There is a robust flow of candid information. Management actively gathers and provides accurate, ongoing feedback. There are many formal and informal channels of communication between units. Employees are encouraged to raise questions and concerns, and offer possible solutions. All ideas are welcomed and evaluated on their merits irrespective of source. Rumors are kept to a minimum because there is not much of an information vacuum to fill. When rumors occur, they are quickly detected and addressed.

FIELD NOTES:

Information flow is most critical within an organization—and most highly sought—when things are changing. At such times, it may be the organization's single most valuable commodity.

Trust

Toxic: Candid feedback is minimal because of distrust among supervisors and employees and among different units. The first response to any problem is usually denial because failure is penalized and candor is not rewarded. There tends to be a lot of blaming and finger pointing.

Ideas may get co-opted or simply ignored. People are not trusted to make decisions on their own, so they learn not to.

Healthy: People feel comfortable sharing information because trust levels are high. Mistakes are quickly acknowledged and addressed because management values the lessons learned.

New ideas are appreciated. People feel respected for their contributions, so they are eager to contribute.

FIELD NOTES:

Reward the behavior you want to see—and model it.

Thinking Sets the Environment

Just as with Clockwise and Counterclockwise Thinking, the contrast between a healthy innovation environment and a toxic one can be stark. In many organizations the toxic environment looks more familiar. In others the two are blended, depending on where you are in the organization and the issue at hand. Rarely is a healthy environment the case on a broad scale, for the same reasons that Clockwise Thinking is so often exceptional: We have long been conditioned to think and behave in certain ways.

No wonder change is so often difficult!

A toxic innovation environment is a logical extension of Counterclockwise Thinking. When we become convinced that we have figured things out (or someone has done that for us) then it makes perfect sense to insist that everyone do things in a predetermined way. If the goal is knowledge then taking credit for the ideas of others is likely to be rewarded. If there are right and wrong ways to do things, then why would you want to change something that's working?

With Counterclockwise Thinking, whoever knows the most is considered the smartest. So, ambitious employees gather as much information as possible and share as little of it as possible with potential rivals. Being wrong is unacceptable, so any hint of error must be denied. Making changes is just not worth the risk.

Counterclockwise Thinking drives an entirely different set of strategies than Clockwise Thinking, and they are not strategies to be proud of. They include: avoid risk, guard information, reject new opinions, deny mistakes, and resist change. Yet in the type of environment created by Counterclockwise Thinking those strategies are perfectly rational.

In other words, Clockwise and Counterclockwise Thinking are each self-reinforcing—which happens to be one of the characteristics of feedback loops. The good news is that when Counterclockwise Thinking is shifted to Clockwise, those new patterns can become self-sustaining. The mere habit of thinking Clockwise makes us more creative. That's why creative people tend to have many creative ideas.

Clockwise Thinking is also self-sustaining within a company. This is especially true when communication becomes so candid that people have the freedom to call each other (politely) on the patterns they use and have the vocabulary to describe it. Everyone self-monitors and respectfully keeps a check on each other, forming a web of self-reinforcing feedback loops.

FIELD NOTES:

Even open-mindedness and tolerance are sometimes treated as counterclockwise skills. They can be just as driven by rules as intolerance and prejudice. As we embrace positive values, we need to be cautious that we don't treat them as an alternative dogma (e.g. political correctness).

The Clockwise Organization

One of the fascinating things about Clockwise Thinking is that it is scalable. Just as individuals can choose to think Clockwise, so can companies and other organizations. The more people you have asking questions and conducting experiments, the faster you can find solutions.

Just one person thinking Clockwise inside a company can reap benefits, but when everyone does it, its power grows exponentially—like an explosion. Innovative Leadership is about creating the sort of environment that allows that to happen.

While Clockwise Thinking alone does not necessarily create a healthy innovation environment, you can't build a healthy environment until you get people to begin thinking Clockwise. To be effective on an organizational level you need both. People need to understand how to begin thinking Clockwise and they need to be encouraged to do it.

Unfortunately, Counterclockwise management techniques are just as ingrained as Counterclockwise Thinking. They are not easy to overcome, but the effort is well worth it, and the potential payoff is massive.

Command and Control

What too often passes for leadership is nothing more than command and control. It is simply exercising authority over people, which works fine if you're content to think and act Counterclockwise. When the goal is simply to maintain the status quo, command and control works just fine. If everything has been figured out and there is no need to change, then all you need is a conductor—if that. If all the employees know their jobs and are willing to continue doing them as they have in the past, even command and control is barely necessary.

Few of us would call that leadership. We expect leaders to implement change, to take the organization somewhere, to at least help it weather the storms that inevitably hit. Otherwise the support staff and the accounting department could maintain control without any need for management.

Even when change is the plan, the techniques used to implement it are usually those developed to reinforce old-fashioned command and control. Creative thinking is only permitted at the top—if even there. Everyone else is simply ordered to follow.

Command and control works pretty well when everything is stable. In the past, when technology and markets changed slowly, the lack of flexibility that command and control creates was less of a problem. When it's used to manage a poorly educated work force, it may even have advantages. But those things don't characterize most businesses today.

There will always be a place for some command and control, just as organizations require some closed feedback loops. But fostering innovation means keeping it to a minimum and tempering it in many ways.

FIELD NOTES:

Command and control is the leadership model that logically flows from Counterclockwise Thinking.

Innovative Leadership Attributes

⟳ Innovative Leadership . . .

Practices Clockwise Values

Innovative Leadership rewards effort. It encourages thoughtful risk taking and experimentation. It considers employees to be crucial business assets because they are the source of all insights. There is a willingness to invest in the company's human capital through training and experience, with an emphasis on thinking creatively and developing new ideas.

Managers model and encourage healthy Clockwise values that include courage, integrity, and independent thinking. Failure is recognized as a necessary part of the process of gaining useful insights. The emphasis is on learning from setbacks rather than avoiding them entirely. Diversity is considered a competitive advantage because it provides a source of many potential solutions that otherwise might not be found.

Under command and control, management focuses almost exclusively on results. It strives to minimize or eliminate risk and views employees as a necessary cost of doing business. Managers expect loyalty, conformity, and performance as defined by detailed job descriptions. Values are set at the top and may not be well articulated to employees. Or the organization's values have evolved by default without careful consideration, following predictable Counterclockwise patterns. Diversity may be recognized as a social good, but one with little tangible business value.

↻ Innovative Leadership . . .

Maintains Strong Communications

Healthy information flow is imperative to promoting the greatest possible number of creative connections. There is strong top-down information flow. Management is focused on making sure everyone knows what's happening. High-level decisions are quickly disseminated, limited only by competitive concerns. Even those concerns are weighed against the advantages of keeping employees informed and engaged.

There is also a strong information flow from the bottom up. Employee input on business decisions is sought and encouraged so no good idea is overlooked. Managers recognize that the best solutions frequently come from whoever is closest to the problem.

Under command and control, information is hoarded, then shared only when deemed absolutely necessary to complete tasks. Orders are passed down the chain of command but other information flow from management to employees is usually an afterthought and a low priority. Employees feel disconnected from management and from the organization's larger objectives. Management has little access to information from employees who are usually closest to the problem and to the customer.

↺ Innovative Leadership ...

Has a Well-Articulated Mission

Innovative Leadership understands the crucial importance of a clear vision. The value of strategic thinking and planning is not just that it provides a long-term perspective. It's that it provides the criteria to evaluate ideas and actions in real time, guiding decisions as they have to be made throughout the organization each day.

Managers actively seek input and strive to define a shared vision, so people recognize the value and impact of their work and want to contribute. Those objectives should be as visible and tangible and compelling as possible, to literally *capture* everyone's imagination in the pursuit of those objectives. Expected outcomes are kept deliberately broad and inclusive, so as not to discourage new ideas and approaches.

Under Counterclockwise command and control, management dictates the organization's mission, sometimes on an *ad hoc* basis. Counterclockwise Thinking means new ideas are filtered based on whether they directly reinforce management's objectives—even though those objectives may not be clear. Because the emphasis is on screening ideas, any lack of clarity tends to eliminate ideas that might in fact be helpful, and discourages people from offering their ideas.

FIELD NOTES:

People can be persuaded to do all sorts of things when you control their paycheck. That may get the job done but it's not leadership.

↻ Innovative Leadership . . .

Charts a Unique Course

In a dynamic business environment, what worked yesterday may not work today, much less tomorrow. So looking at what others have done successfully, while helpful, is no guarantee of future success. A company would be unwise to try to reverse engineer what Microsoft has done and try to follow that path. Not only because Microsoft is already here but because the unique circumstances, dynamics, and patterns that led to Microsoft's success no longer exist. If it were easy to copy that sort of success, we would all be very rich. The environment has changed.

That does not mean it's not worthwhile to emulate other companies and individuals, but thinking Clockwise means treating them as a source of possibilities, not directives. Instead of Best Management Practices, we need to talk about Best Management *Principles* (as this book does). Innovative Leadership seeks to identify the broad principles that promote success, while adapting and readapting them to the circumstances at hand.

FIELD NOTES:

Much of what worked in the past is virtually guaranteed not to work in the future.

↺ Innovative Leadership . . .

Expects Repercussions

An Innovative Leader recognizes that his or her actions inevitably prompt reactions. Cause and effect flow both ways. Everyone involved, including employees, supervisors, unions, customers, suppliers, stockholders, and the larger community all exert influence. A simple edict rarely has simple consequences. Threatening discipline if employees do not do purchase orders according to strict procedures may reduce errors. However, it may also dramatically slow down the processing of all purchase orders, creating delays and even bigger problems than the original edict sought to solve.

Feedback patterns sometimes lead to exactly the opposite effect of what is intended. A policy of taking back any leftover dollars at the end of each budget cycle creates a powerful incentive to make sure no dollars are left. Penalizing customers for late payments may make them pay more promptly, or it may drive customers away. Insisting on strict secrecy often promotes rumors and leaks.

Innovative Leadership means keeping the larger goals in mind and striving to anticipate how those interactions play out, so as to minimize unintended consequences.

> FIELD NOTES:
>
> Command and control is frequently ineffective at even maintaining the status quo.

↻ Innovative Leadership . . .

Actively Seeks Feedback

Management actively seeks accurate feedback on all aspects of the operation—including feedback from employees and from outside stakeholders such as customers and suppliers. That data is used to measure the success of ongoing operations and innovation experiments. It's gathered conscientiously and carefully analyzed to guide business decisions. Managers model this value by seeking feedback on their own performance and interactions.

In a Command and Control culture, management wants to know what's happening, but may be indifferent to tracking any data other than the hard numbers that measure output and performance, or what may be needed to address a problem.

When there is no well-defined infrastructure for gathering and sharing information, meaningful feedback is often hard to obtain and unreliable. That may reinforce a tendency under command and control to ignore feedback because it's not worth the trouble, or because it's obsolete by the time it has been gathered.

Business metrics and accounting are critical tools, not only as ways to measure performance and maintain control, but to provide important and powerful feedback into a Clockwise loop.

This changes the role and emphasis of some parts of the organization. For example, bookkeeping and accounting are used less as ways to monitor and control and more as communications and feedback links.

Management needs to be highly proactive and visible about using feedback to find positive solutions, not just keep score. The data will always be incomplete and horded until people are convinced that it's in their interest to provide it rather than withhold it.

FIELD NOTES:

Management does not need to have all the right answers as much as it needs to ask the right questions.

↻ Innovative Leadership . . .

Routinely Redefines Success

If feedback is taken seriously, there will be times when it points in new directions, when the clearest path to success changes. Innovative Leadership is always alert to that possibility. Management is prepared to make course corrections or to even rethink strategic objectives as needed. By constantly being on alert, managers detect market trends early when it's easier to respond effectively—or even anticipate changes before they occur.

Change is embraced as healthy and inevitable. Improvisation is considered a routine business practice that is applied to everything from business processes to product lines to customer and vendor relationships. Business practices and strategies are constantly subject to review and revision, due to changing circumstances and in light of fresh insights.

↻ Innovative Leadership . . .

Sets Thoughtful Boundaries

Managers strive to set only those limits that are necessary to keep the organization on track. That way leaders influence decisions and manage risks while allowing for creative improvements and fresh approaches.

Policies are carefully designed to create appropriate incentives and rewards. Management sets boundaries and then allows units and employees considerable discretion within those boundaries, while measuring performance. Where it's not feasible to allow employees much latitude, such as on an assembly line or in accounting, suggested improvements are actively sought and considered for implementation.

With command and control, policies are designed primarily to maintain control and authority, and to assure that things get done correctly. Management prescribes jobs and procedures and requires permission in advance for any exceptions. There is a lot of standardization throughout the organization, but that is not necessarily driven by any needs other than administrative. Whenever there is a problem, the solution is applied broadly in an effort to maintain fairness and consistency. That often happens without carefully considering whether the same solution is appropriate in every situation.

FIELD NOTES:

Insisting on consistency can be just as arbitrary and unfair as having no consistency.

↻ Innovative Leadership . . .

Coaches

When we think Clockwise and uphold those values, we recognize that our ideas are not certainties, so we offer them as suggestions and possibilities.

In any organization, experience has value. Prior knowledge is important because it tells us where the land mines are. The challenge is to use that knowledge without allowing it to restrict new approaches. So innovative leaders refrain from proclaiming what won't work—even when that has been the experience in the past. Instead, they use those experiences to formulate relevant questions like,

"Have you thought about . . . ?" or,

"How will you account for . . . ?" or,

"Have you figured out how to address . . . ?" or,

"Are you aware that . . . ?"

That saves someone from repeating past mistakes while leaving them free to discover new and better solutions.

FIELD NOTES:

Thinking Clockwise is what makes someone coach-able because that person isn't locked into a set way of doing things.

🕁 Innovative Leadership . . .

Accepts Failure

Managers understand that failure is necessary to progress. Every idea that doesn't work brings the organization closer to one that does. So managers are allowed to fail and they allow employees to fail as long as the task is not so critical that failure will jeopardize the enterprise.

This is not to say that normal business objectives are abandoned. Ultimate success and efficiency are as important as ever, but there is recognition that thoughtful experimentation is an important step to getting there.

Instead of avoiding experimentation, managers need to be adept at managing it to minimize the cost and potential disruption. They should use it to find answers as quickly and efficiently as possible. Experimentation needs to be undertaken early in projects while the resource commitment is relatively small. Frequent small experiments are usually less risky than infrequent large ones. The lessons learned are seen as a benefit to be used as soon as possible.

Experimentation and discretion are closely related. When there is a degree of latitude allowed, solutions or improvements can be tried on a small scale, and then expanded if they prove worthwhile. Effective managers maintain flexibility while setting prudent boundaries so things don't "fall off the table."

Counterclockwise organizations experiment, too. Any new product or process is inevitably a test. But when there is a reluctance to acknowledge real experimentation, it tends to get delayed until the stakes are so high that failure is catastrophic. Then, in typical Counterclockwise fashion, bad news is rejected, denied, or manipulated until problems become inescapable—and expensive.

FIELD NOTES:

We progress when we're able to systematically try new things, while retaining whatever works. To sustain our progress we must recognize that what works changes over time. So we must constantly invent new solutions.

◔ Innovative Leadership . . .

Builds Trust

Management is careful to give credit where it's due. So employees, teams, and units feel recognized and rewarded for their efforts and ideas. Discipline is generally avoided in favor of coaching and mentoring. There is a culture of pulling together to solve problems and face challenges. This makes employees more willing to be candid about what's working and what's not.

Command and control management believes its primary trust is to get the job done "right." Any variation from management's orders is cause for suspicion or discipline. Business data is used almost exclusively to catch problems and shortfalls—or when the news is good, to puff up management. Employees become conditioned to avoid criticism by providing only the information they are required to provide.

When trust levels are low, it is difficult to gather the kind of data that accurately reveals problems, weaknesses, and their causes. Without that data, problems fester and grow and resources are wasted on the wrong potential solutions.

FIELD NOTES:

The time-honored practice of management by exception can severely undermine trust. If employees only get attention when they do something wrong, they will stop taking risks or volunteering information.

Finding Balance

The natural world strikes a balance between open and closed feedback loops, using each when it's appropriate. When the skin is cut, the body uses chemical signals to create a positive feedback loop that tells the platelets in our blood to become "sticky" and join together to form a scab to stop the bleeding. Once the scab has been formed, the body must send negative signals to halt that loop; otherwise, blood throughout the body would gradually coagulate.

Any society must have ways to maintain acceptable behaviors by creating negative feedback loops in the community (e.g. the criminal justice system) and teaching citizens to self-regulate behavior within appropriate limits. This is one of the roles both parents and schools have always played. The problem comes when those norms are no longer treated as boundaries and instead become rigid requirements for how everyone should think and behave.

It's the same in a business or government or any organization. There will always need to be some level of negative feedback (such as requiring people to work in order to be paid). But when too many behaviors are prescribed, there is no room for experimentation or modeling new possibilities. So there is no innovation. The trick is to maintain those closed feedback loops that are necessary to sustain success, without dampening the explosions that fuel innovation.

However, the interplay between these two patterns is an organizational dynamic, not a personal one. That is to say that some closed-loop Counterclockwise *mechanisms* are important to the functioning of a business, organization, or society. Counterclockwise is not a necessary or helpful way to *think*. We should always be striving to *think* Clockwise.

The Big Stuff

Many of the most promising innovations involve more elements than any one employee or unit is capable of implementing. The required time and resources are too great. The changes required are too complex. Yet, it may be something of tremendous potential value to the enterprise. It might be a new product line, or a restructuring of customer or vendor relationships.

Under such circumstances, a Counterclockwise culture creates still more obstacles. It promotes a reluctance to ask the hard questions and to do the experimentation necessary to answer them. It tends to discount promising possibilities for the wrong reasons. Too often, it is simply blind to crucial facts and insights.

In a Clockwise culture the whole process of evaluating and implementing ideas is enhanced. If you have a promising proposal to make, who would you rather make it to: someone who already thinks they know it all and resists change, or someone who is curious, pragmatic, and constantly open to new possibilities? If it was your money about to be invested, who would you want making that decision? Whatever your perspective may be, Clockwise Thinking leads to better decisions.

FIELD NOTES:

Clockwise and Counterclockwise Thinking are, at their core, decision making processes.

Added Benefits

So far innovation has been the central emphasis of Innovative Leadership but it is certainly not the only benefit. When we create a culture of experimentation and imagination, we are permitting people to do what they did when they were babies. We are allowing them to play with ideas and make discoveries. It is what our minds were programmed to do and it is a joyful experience.

The fun part of any job is not following some routine laid down for us; it is taking on new challenges, using our creativity and skills, and getting recognition for our insights. When we allow people to do that, we are making them more productive while building satisfaction, loyalty, and commitment.

Isn't that what real leadership is supposed to accomplish?

Innovative Leadership is in reality a model for *effective* leadership. Counterclockwise Thinking only works when everything is completely static and unchanging—and not always then. Only by thinking Clockwise do we gain the dynamic adaptability we need to keep even our *unchanging* plans on track despite changing circumstances

---

FIELD NOTES:

Sometimes we need to adapt in order to keep things as they are.

Mechanisms for accountability are a hallmark of command and control. They assure that orders are followed. Accountability is also important under Innovative Leadership, but it means something a little different. In that context, it means holding people accountable for Clockwise values and practices.

Creating a Clockwise culture, by definition, requires everyone's active participation. Those who insist on arbitrarily controlling the flow of information create bottlenecks and confusion. Those unwilling to take prudent risks fail to conduct important experiments, and will not permit others to do so. Those who co-opt ideas destroy trust.

Counterclockwise attitudes are counterproductive, so they have to be addressed. Breaking those old patterns needs to become a performance issue. Clockwise accountability means insisting that everyone assume responsibility for the whole enterprise, pulling in the same direction and trusting Clockwise Thinking enough to let it run its course.

If everyone understands the new rules of the game and believes that the organization as a whole truly embraces those rules, people are empowered. There is a natural tendency to reinforce the Clockwise behaviors and discourage the Counterclockwise ones.

FIELD NOTES:

Part of Clockwise Thinking is a willingness to accept valid feedback and act on it.

In the natural world, when you put a healthy seed into an appropriate environment, growth is assured. Ideas work the same way. With the right idea and the right circumstances, success is guaranteed. The challenge is finding the right idea and creating those circumstances.

Coming up with that great insight is a process of thoughtful experimentation—which is what Clockwise Thinking requires. Creating the right environment is the role of Innovative Leadership. When we combine the two, success is inevitable.

> ### FIELD NOTES:
>
> Success, in business as in life, must be discovered— and constantly rediscovered.

Just as Innovative Leadership is based on Clockwise Thinking, practicing Clockwise Thinking tends to make us Innovative Leaders. Whenever we embrace new ideas, approaches and improvements, we define ourselves as leaders no matter where we are in the hierarchy of an organization. The nature of feedback is such that it can be effectively initiated in many ways and from a variety of sources. When we change our individual behaviors, we inevitably create ripples of change in those around us.

To begin that process, I suggest you go to www.ThinkClockwise.com. There, you can take a self-evaluation quiz that will help you determine what combination of Clockwise and Counterclockwise Thinking you tend to use. You'll also find a place to leave comments, questions, and insights, as well as links to other information and resources. I urge you to apply Clockwise Thinking to all areas of your life, and I would love to hear about your experiences with it.

Think Clockwise.